Silent Voices

MARILYN L. THOMPSON

CONTENTS

INTRODUCTION

The purpose of this book is to increase awareness of how our mental health is connected to our physical health. The World Health Organization (WHO) defines mental health as a condition subject to fluctuations due to biological and social factors that enable an individual to form and maintain harmonious relations with others and to participate in constructive changes in his or her social and physical environment. It also enables an individual to form and maintain relations with his or herself as well.

Simone Biles' mental health affecting her physical ability at the 2020 Summer Olympics in Tokyo is an example of how our mental health functions can affect our physical health functions. Mental health involves our daily effective functioning: productive activities, healthy relationships, and ability to adapt to change. Mental health reflects our emotional, psychological, and social well-being: how we think, feel, and act. *Silent Voices* will bring awareness to some mental health issues as disabled seniors express how their physical health affects their mental health. Physical health and mental health go hand in hand.

This is not a religious book, but it is faith based. Many disabled seniors correlate mental health with their faith. In other words, they find mental stability through their personal faith. Come, journey with me and hear the voices of some disabled seniors crying out in the wilderness while becoming aware of the challenges they endure on a daily basis. You will read of disabled seniors breaking their silence to bring awareness to things that affect their mental and physical well-being. A peek into their lives will help explain why awareness of the outlined issues is necessary.

The voices of disabled seniors depicted in this book often center around their faith. However, we all have some form of beliefs which influence us.

We must ask the following questions:

- What is faith?

- Do you have strong faith, one that carries you through life's challenges and curveballs?

- Do you have a false sense of faith?

According to the *Stanford Encyclopedia of Philosophy*, faith has three components: the affective, the cognitive, and the practical. Faith is usually based on the religion people practice, which includes, but is not limited to, a range of different concepts:

- Christians: faith is in Jesus Christ, and believe Jesus Christ is the Son of God.

- Muslims: faith is in the Honorable Muhammad, and believe in Abu al-Qasim Muhammad ibn 'Abd Allah ibn 'Abd al-Muttalib ibn Hashim is God's Prophet.

- Some have faith in Buddha, one who achieved supreme enlightenment.

Simply put, faith is when you trust or believe in something very strongly.

For example: God is the starting point, and the source of our lives. In other words, "God is the potter, and we are the clay."(Holy Bible: Isaiah 64: 8).

Faith is also the substance of things hoped for without evidence.

The book will also bring awareness to unusual abuse or neglect of disabled seniors, the kinds most people don't know about or just don't talk about. The issues discussed are not isolated, they happen more often than you know.

Finally, the voices are crying out: "Stop abusing and neglecting me. I am more than a disability." What is disability? And how are disabled seniors being abuse/neglected?

Physical disability is not the only form of disability affecting seniors. Other forms include emotional, mental, and medical. Remember, disabled seniors are people who deserve to be treated with love, dignity, and respect, regardless of their age or disability. You might become one of those disabled seniors one day. Don't take disabled seniors for granted; disabled senior is both a life and a lifestyle. The young can learn and grow from disabled seniors only if they love, listen, and care.

JUST HEAR ME

One unique issue disabled seniors struggle with is viability (usable, workable, capable; physically and/or mentally fitted to live successfully). In earlier times, it was thought that old age generally sets in at sixty years of age. That was also considered to be a non-viable age. That meant senior citizens were not active enough after reaching that age, therefore they were seen as no longer viable. Disabled seniors often struggle with being seen as non-viable based on their inner feelings or their treatment by others.

Non-viability issues seniors often struggle with can include but are not limited to loneliness, estrangement from family and friends, lack of family interaction or support, poor geriatric facilities (for example: assisted living home, nursing home, or rehabilitation inpatient establishment), as well as a lack of awareness.

Other seniors are seen as marginalized, especially when they are seen only as their physical disability.

Joann

We are viewed as not having mental and physical capacity. I became a prisoner in my own body. When my medical condition started, and at some point during the progression of this condition, I gave up, to some degree. I became embarrassed about my physical appearance; I started feeling like I was a burden to family and friends; and I lost the use of my limbs so I needed assistance with the activities of daily life due to my limited physical capacity. Mentally, however, I continue to grow and am capable of stimulating conversation to contribute my input to the world.

But most of my conversations consist of, How are you today? and What do you want to eat today? Often, I feel like I am just taking up space. Don't just ask me what I want to eat; I want to have a stimulating conversation with substance, without receiving a response like: "Oh, Grandmom, you are just crazy." Elderly is now being equated to being crazy.

I may not be in the world, but I am very much aware of what's going on out there. I have the stigma of being a disabled senior and am treated that way. People think that disabled seniors no longer have the mental or physical capacity to survive as independent agents. Family and friends started to interact with me as if I have lost or limited mental capacity, as well as limited physical capacity.

The definitions of *ableism* and *ageism* explain that people who are described as marginalized are seen as not having the mental or physical capacity to survive as independent agents.

I often ask myself why my physical disability cause me to be seen by others as non-viable. I had always been the glue that kept my family and friends together. Everyone sought out my opinion and came to me for advice. I was the one who coordinated our annual events for family and friends, holiday get-togethers, and so on. However, when I became disabled I noticed that around the dinner table I went from the person I just described to someone that others ignored, including saying things like, "Don't listen to what she is saying." Often I feel unseen, unheard, and unvalued, as though I am just existing. I feel like someone who is learning to swim, but forgot the life jacket. However, I lean on my faith. I find peace by listening to gospel music and focus on the words of the songs. My favorite song is "Precious Lord."

"Precious Lord, take my hand, lead me on so I may stand; through toils and snares I have already come …"

Being viable to me means having the will to live, capability of living, and being able to live, as well as having stimulation of the intellect, imagination, and senses. All I ask of family, friends, and others in general is Please, just hear me. Disabled seniors are slowly becoming a silenced generation. Here I am today, seventy-five years old and with limited physically capacity, but my mental capacity is as strong today as it was when I first became an adult. To marginalize me is to deny me my full rights and status as a citizen of the United States of America. To define us as falling short of the norm disempowers us and excludes us from society.

ABUSE AND NEGLECT

Another issue disabled seniors struggle with is neglect and abuse. I want to bring awareness to a topic that is rarely or never discussed, but is very importance in providing healthy as opposed to unhealthy physical and mental healthcare. Many seniors experience silent emotional suffering, including abandonment, anger, and fear.

Silent emotional suffering means masking, which is covering up stored anger, feelings, and functioning from cognitive distortions and negative perceptions of life-changing events, as well as other people. Many disabled seniors who want to remain in their homes fall victim to silent emotional suffering due to neglect or abuse. Nevertheless, excuses are made for the responsible family member's attitude and behavior, and the neglect or abuse goes unreported or unsubstantiated if it is reported.

This topic will also bring awareness to seniors residing in assisted-living facilities and those who have caregivers hired by home healthcare agencies, who take financial advantage of the senior by whatever means are available to them. This type of neglect or abuse often goes unreported.

HELP, SOMEBODY, PLEASE

Debra

*I**am a disabled senior who is trying to appear emotionally
strong, but it is a cover up. Silently, I am suffering emotionally. I just try to live, day by day, the best way I can. It has been
a long, thirty-year journey to accept my physical disability.
However, I continue to struggle with having to explain how I
became disabled, coupled with my physical appearance. It continues to be embarrassing because people greet me in public as
if I am my physical disability, not a functioning person.*

From the bottom of my heart to the depths of my soul, I believe I
am supposed to be dead, sleeping in my grave, but God made death stand
back and behave. My first traumatic life-changing event was the day I was
gunned down.

When my incident first happened, I was attending church. I grew up in the church. I believed and still do in God. However, on that day my faith was shattered. I did not know why this was happening to me. During this time, my church friends told me that God was going to heal me and I would walk again. I really believed them and put my faith in them. This kept me going for years, each day believing that one day I was going to walk. I have been paralyzed, in my bed and in my wheelchair, for thirty years after being shot by my ex-boyfriend. He is the father of my only child. After returning home from vacation, life threw me a curveball that I did not see coming. My life changed in an instant, and my faith was tested. I developed a false sense of faith after being shot and paralyzed. I had just turned thirty-eight years old one week before, and my child was three years old. I lost so much that day, including my self-worth and my self-value.

I had to raise my child as a disabled single parent. My daughter always had a love/hate relationship toward me. She was a defiant child, and blamed me for her not having a relationship with her father, who was in prison. You see, I was not the only person he shot that day. He also went to his son's mother's house and shot her as well.

I started parenting from a false sense of guilt and using impaired judgment. I knew being shot was not my fault, but I was made to feel that it was. Anger controlled my attitude, behavior, thoughts, and feelings for years. Being shot and paralyzed left me physically, mentally, and emotionally scarred for life.

I have suffered from depression and anxiety for years, sometimes on a daily basis. I am now sixty-eight years old, and my condition is such that I need others to physically assist me.

My second life-changing event is becoming dependent on my daughter. You see, in order to stay in my home, my daughter and her two children had to live with me. However, our constant conflict continues, resulting in poor home healthcare and daily neglect and verbal abuse. I am treated as if I am a burden, with no dignity or self-worth.

A third life-changing event occurred upon my ex's release from prison. My daughter insisted that she and her daughters have a relationship with him. Therefore, I silently suffer by masking my unspoken anger and fear of him.

My daughter allows him to come over to my home, take the grandchildren out, and bring them things. He acts as if nothing has happened, and I pretend everything is okay. I feel trapped, a prisoner in my own home. He has never apologized to me, yet he is walking around free and I remain a prisoner in my bed, paralyzed from the waist down. I was robbed of doing things with my grandchildren, such as taking them places, going out to eat, and attending events like graduations, and so on.

On the one hand, I know God loves me, and He helps me with my faith, struggles, anger, and fears. I have finally accepted that I will never be able to walk again.

On the other hand, I am ready to break my silence and speak out about the neglect and abuse I've endured from my daughter. Breaking my silence may help other disabled seniors who are being neglected or abused by a family member speak out.

I am nothing more than a means for my daughter to get her needs met. I have the resources, house, and income, as do many other disabled seniors who are living in their own homes. I now have come to terms with my past failed efforts to maintain as much independence for as long as I can. I am fed up with my daughter's neglect and abuse, but it is hard to put her out since she established residency by receiving mail at my address. She also threatens to take my grandchildren away, and my sixteen-year-old granddaughter is the one who assists me with getting my needs met at home. This could lead to me facing a fourth life-changing event. I fear being abandoned. What will happen to me? Therefore, I continue to suffer, silently and in fear. My daughter's ongoing neglect and verbal abuse puts my safety and welfare at risk, and I must accept it is not in my best interest for my daughter and I to continue living together. It is time to separate and find alternative living arrangements.

I do not qualify for assisted living because I cannot transfer independently from my bed to my wheelchair. I no longer qualify for Medicaid, therefore I cannot afford home healthcare services provided by the state.

Jeff

From my childhood to my teenage years, I had mental health issues that went unmentioned, unnoticed, and untreated, and I was physically, emotionally, and sexually abused. I did not like myself, and I was depressed all the time. I ran away from home at age fifteen and moved in with a trusted family member who sexually abused me for several years. I have kept my sexual abuse a secret until now. As I approached adulthood, I started living a lie. I was obsessed with not becoming a loser, and proving to myself that I was a heterosexual male. I married three times, and was known as a Casanova.

Then life threw me a curveball. At age thirty-seven, I lost my job when I was terminated for sexual harassment. During the same year, I suffered kidney failure and needed a kidney transplant. My third wife left me and filed for divorce. I sank deeper and deeper into depression, with thoughts of suicide on a daily basis. I cut myself off from family and friends. There were many days when I just sat with a gun to my head or in my mouth, wanting to end my suffering, but I could not pull the trigger. I started isolating more and more.

At this dark time in my life, I had lost my sense of faith or I had no faith at all.

SEXUAL EXPLOITATION

Sexual exploitation is another issue facing disabled male seniors, but most are silent on this issue. Exploitation is the illegal use or wasting of money, property, or other assets of a protected person who is physically or mentally unable to make decisions or care for themselves. According to Swarthmore College's Sexual Harassment / Assault Resources and Education (SHARE) sexual exploitation is defined as an act or acts committed through the exploitation of another person's sexuality for the purpose of financial gain and personal benefit or advantage.

Jeff

I am a sixty-year-old male with kidney functioning rated at ten and below. I must break my silence regarding the abuse of disabled males, which is never talked about. Abuse or neglect sometimes happens within the actual delivery of services, and often goes unreported to the governing body responsible for providing the service.

My first two experiences were traumatic. I did not know what to do, therefore I fell victim to sexual exploitation. I kept silent, first because I did not want to get the worker fired, and second because I was so confused. My judgment was impaired because of my own perception of my life. After the first few weeks of services, the caregiver started telling me all of her family and financial problems. Since I liked and appreciated what she was doing to help me, I started giving her advice about her family situation. Then she started asking me for money on a weekly basis, making excuses for not showing up to work or coming late. I started experiencing increased anxiety, until I spoke out several months later during a therapy session. I told about what was happening to me, and I was encouraged to report her to the home healthcare agency. The young lady was quickly replaced. However, my second caregiver also started telling me her financial and family problems after a couple weeks of working. I listened, but offered no advice. After a few weeks with the second caregiver, I was sitting in my living room and she was cleaning my bathroom. She came out of my bathroom naked, and offered to have sex.

I was in disbelief. I had not seen a naked women in many years, and I suffered a severe panic attack. I started sweating profusely, became confused, had flashbacks of past sexual harassment charges, and became very fearful. My blood pressure went up. I thought I shouldn't feel this way. I asked the young lady to put her clothes on. My therapy session was the next day, and I was a nervous wreck. I became aware; I had a panic attack, and the affect the caregiver's act had on my emotions and mental health. Her act woke up desires I had not felt in years, and I started wanting to have a relationship with a woman again. But, I felt violated after learning that sexual exploitation is a form of abuse. I was encouraged to report the caregiver's act to the healthcare agency. She was immediately replaced.

Bobby

Becoming a sugar daddy is another classic example of sexual exploitation that happens to some disabled seniors. I am an eighty-eight-year-old widowed man who resides in assisted living housing. I have the freedom to come and come as I please, however my children help with making decisions on my behalf. My wife died a few years ago, and now I'm lonely and want a girlfriend.

One day, while I was around and about in the community, I met a forty-eight-year-old woman who has four children. She was faced with housing hardships. I explained that I resided in assisted living, but she could move in with me for thirty days before she would have to move out based on the rules of the facility. So, she moved in with me and became my girlfriend. I can't tell my children about her, they won't understand.

After she secured her own housing, I help pay her bills whenever I can. She tells me that if I don't give her money when she asks I cannot call her or see her. When I don't have the money to help her, I become very confused and stressed, not knowing what to do. I don't want to lose her.

Even though a high percentage of caregivers do not engage in sexually exploitative acts, sexual exploitation happens regularly. This is why we must talk about it: to raise awareness. These men are vulnerable, which makes it very easy for women to prey on them for financial gain. This happens to both poor and moderate-income disabled seniors alike. However, the disabled senior often does not see this act as a problem. Many see it as an opportunity to receive some form of pleasure, making them think, *I still got it!* Remember, disabled males continue to have sexual thoughts and desires, regardless of their physical, mental, or medical circumstances. But, there are certain boundaries caregivers should not cross. Caregivers must be held accountable, and adhere to both moral and ethical obligations.

The next cases represent type of exploitative abuse that some home healthcare system administrators know exist, but do not talk about. The issue is caregivers using the disabled senior's debit or credit card for personal gain, as well as unauthorized bank withdrawals. This is happening too often to disabled seniors who depend on this service.

Will

I am a seventy-six-year-old blind male who receives state-funded home healthcare services. I have had several caregivers who have taken financial advantage of me. I need caregiver services seven days a week. The caregiver services include food shopping and running errands. I must give the worker my debit card so they can do these things for me. However, some workers use my card to pay for their own groceries, as well as mine. I've also had caregivers take money out of my bank account without my permission. A few have charged me extra for gas for their vehicles, even when using their car is part of the agency's services. Not all home healthcare agencies offer transportation to run errands. Transportation is essential for me, so I can shop for food and run other errands. I am helpless in many ways and need the assistance, but I do not deserve to be taken advantage of. You see, I am on a fixed income, and need every penny to continue surviving day by day.

Karen

I am a seventy-seven-year-old woman in assisted living housing. I receive home healthcare services funded by the state. I am speaking out regarding caseworkers using my debit card for their own personal use. The staff thinks I am paranoid when I report various incidents.

Before moving into assisted living, I had my own home with nice, valuable things. I moved some of my furniture and valuables with me. My valuable silverware was exchanged for old silverware. The caseworker thought I did not know the difference. For several months, this caseworker used my debit card for her personal gain while food shopping for me. She was reported for stealing my money, and was immediately replaced.

Joyce

I am a seventy-year-old blind female in assisted living housing that is not funded by the Department of Housing and Urban Development. I have to pay out of pocket due to my moderate income. My husband and I lived well and were socialites in our community. After his death, I lost sight in my right eye completely, and am losing sight in my left eye as well. I also became medically disabled. I needed to downsize, therefore I moved into assisted living.

I am speaking out because I am constantly violated by the staff of the facility where I reside. I am labeled a complainer, therefore, I am mostly ignored when I complain. I have had many items stolen from my apartment. When I complain of stolen property, staff respond as if I have memory loss and do not believe me. I decided to put cameras in my apartment. The maintenance man was caught on camera stealing my jewelry and other items such as valuable purses. When he was reported with evidence, the maintenance man was fired. I just want to be heard and believed.

The home healthcare system often handles this problem by replacing the worker. Often, no reports are made to authorities such as the police.

EFFECTS OF COVID-19

March 2020 became one of the most devastating, life-changing event to happen in our lifetimes. COVID-19 threw the world a curveball that we did not see coming. The world became temporarily disabled/handicapped. People were getting sick and dying, there were no funerals for loved ones, there were mass burials, hospital respirators were in great demand, quarantines were put in place, masks had to be worn, the economic system was affected. In fact, all systems that provided services were crippled.

COVID-19 affected the world, and the unknown effects of this virus had a profound effect on everyone, especially disabled seniors. Many died alone, confused about what was happening; others struggled with fear and loneliness, which increased anxiety, depression, and end-of-life concerns. Some disable seniors living in their own homes feared having to be hospitalized.

Disabled seniors in nursing homes were affected in ways that were previously unimaginable. Many died from COVID-19. In 2021, the Delta variant affected the world the same way COVID-19 had, and unvaccinated nursing home staff put nursing home residents at a higher risk of contracting the virus. Cases of the Delta variant soared due to high numbers of unvaccinated, and warnings of things getting worse caused a much quicker response from government officials. Mandatory vaccinations for healthcare workers were implemented.

By the end of 2021, another variant, Omicron, affected the world. The variants, coupled with controversy over wearing masks and mandated vaccinations, put disabled seniors residing in senior-care facilities at higher risk. Many disabled seniors in senior care facility lost their lives. COVID-19 may have exacerbated or affected their medical conditions in some way. Nevertheless, COVID-19 deaths in these types of facilities often went unreported.

TRANSITIONING

Mental health has advanced in many ways, but there is so much more that can be learned to help us understand how our mental health affects our body, mind, and soul. When disabled seniors approach this stage of life, it leads to questions like: What is going to happen to me once I die?

A therapeutic Socratic approach is useful to help the individual examine their belief system, which addresses life after death. Some belief systems do not believe in life after death, but others do. For those that do, seek knowledge from the Holy Bible or other religion-based books (spiritual books of faith).

For we do not know the time nor the hour our body will fail. As one senior worded it, "for I know my body will fail, as quick as tomorrow."

The question of what will happen when someone dies leads to end-of-life concerns that a lot of people struggle with, but they share the same emotional and psychological concerns that affect the person's mental health, including the body, mind, and soul.

Examples of expressed end-of-life concerns include:

The world is going nuts. I am glad I won't be around to live in it, but my child will, and I worry if she will be able to survive. I practice no religious beliefs, but believe in being an upright citizen: I have done what I am supposed to do, I went to college, worked hard, have a good family and friends, and I am financially secure. However, is this all there is to life? Was it all worth it? I believe that once we die, that is the end. I just hope I do not die a hater of other people, based on my opinion of their race or ethnicity.

B "HELL", does it really exist? Does the end mean just that "The End"? Sometimes I feel like I'm living in hell on earth.

Willie

I am a sixty-eight-year-old man who lived a hard life, going against all odds my entire life. I lived by the hard knocks of the streets. I had to struggle and survive life's curveballs, kicks, knocks, bruises, and scares the best and only ways I knew. I was in my early sixties, but appeared much older and was terminally ill when my caseworker referred me for counseling. I was struggling with severe medical problems, as well as suffering from severe depression and high anxiety.

Upon entering therapy, Willie expressed, "I want to get my life together, and, how does the Bible instruct a man about his duty and commitment to his wife?" I was having severe marital problems during this time, and everyone was telling me to leave my wife of many years. This had me very depressed and very stressed, coupled with my health issues. My body, mind, and soul were afflicted. However, I started attending church, clinging on to every word the minister said. (Working on his mind.) My mind started reconnecting to the teachings of my grandmother in relation to God. I started nourishing the inner man, (my soul). This gave me hope in hopeless situations, as well as a will to live. I became interested in staying active and strong. (Working on body.) I developed a thirst for the word of God and the teachings of Scripture. My perception of life and my attitude toward others changed. I started by forgiving individuals who had done or caused Harm to me, as well as forgiving myself for the harm I did or caused to others. I started attending Bible studies in addition to Church. I started witnessing to friends, and leading them to attend church with me. I remained physically, emotionally, and spiritually motivated, and started living a better life for the next five years. However, COVID-19 changed life for everyone, especially for the terminal ill.

Approximately two months before his death, he started missing necessary treatments, which had helped maintain and sustain his life for the last ten plus years. When confronted, he became upset, and said, "I am just tired of going to treatment, loneliness, and isolation." He was struggling with racing thoughts, and thoughts of giving up. COVID-19 had caused America to isolate in order to remain safe. This was necessary, but it was a struggle for many.

On Christmas Day 2021, he was a very sick and weak man. His body was getting weaker, and his mind cloudy. Both body and mind were in pain and suffering. But he focused on nourishing his soul. He wanted to hear something inspirational, like reading scripture, listening to gospel songs, and praying. It appeared that when he did that, he forgot about his pain and suffering. He found a sense of inner peace and unspoken strength. He became very, very humble. The gospel songs he enjoyed that day were from Rance Allen, "You That I Trust" and "Something About the Name Jesus," as well as Tasha Cobb Leonard's "You Know My Name." He began giving praise to God

I really did not know what was happening. Did he know that he was on the verge of dying? What was he experiencing, which will remain his secret? Did he see Azrael (Arabic Izrail or Azrail in Islam), known as the Angel of Death, who appears to the dying to take out their soul? After observing something unexplainable to the human eye, it was clear that something unseen was happening to the inner man. His steadfast faith helped him transition in peace on January 8, 2022.

Sarah

I am an eighty-five-year-old female with chronic dementia who was referred for in-home counseling. I refused to take baths, wash my hair, and communicate with others. I also refused to attend psychiatrist appointments or take psychotropic medication. For the first two sessions, I would not say anything to my therapist, who thought, *How can I help her? How can a rational mind communicate with an irrational mind? What is really happening to the inner self?*

The third session, my therapist focused on the caregiver, who was my daughter. She was experiencing burned-out syndrome. The caregiver explained how she became her mother's caregiver. Her mother's assets was too much to qualify for state assistance. She would have to sell the family house, which the children wanted to inherit. The family decided the daughter would move in with her mother and become sole caregiver. She had been caring for her mother for five years, with no family assistance or support. The daughter herself was in need of respite. She explained that her mother talked to dead people all day, and how this was affecting her. Than the daughter explained why her mother's medical doctor felt she may benefit from counseling. The daughter said her mother was in a coma for several weeks, and her doctor felt end of life was very near. "I was the first to arrive at the hospital to say my goodbye to her, but when I entered the room my mother was reciting a verse from Psalms. I told the doctor what she was reciting. The doctor looked amazed after my mother woke up from her coma. It was like a miracle. She was later released from the hospital.

The daughter wanted me to explain how her mother was able to recite the Word of God while she was unconscious, which the daughter felt had helped her mother come out of her comatose state. She explained that before her mother's current health issues, she was a committed woman of faith, very faithfully serving God, and committed to the local and universal church alike.

I was just as amazed as her doctors after hearing this event. I had no answer. The only explanation I can offer is that Abram believed in God, and God counted him righteous because of his faith. The Word of God is still alive and active, and continues to be sharper than any double-edged sword, penetrating even to dividing soul and spirit, joints and marrow, and discerning the thoughts and intentions of the heart. We all consist of body, mind, and soul. Soul is the spiritual part of humans in its moral aspect, and is nourished through one's faith.

Somewhere in her demented mind, her mother knew her safety and peace was in God. She knew God promised never to leave nor forsake her, and that God would keep her in perfect peace if her mind is stayed on Him, and trusted in Him. Even in her demented state of mind, she remained steadfast in faith. She had the right kind of faith that would take her through to the end, into the afterlife. She remembered God's grace and power, which are amazing.

Doctors were amazed in some ways, and I was amazed in other ways. However, God is Amazing. Her faith can be described as sees the invisible, believes the incredible, and receives the impossible.

I started communicating by having Sarah participate in an activity designed especially for her, a therapeutic Socratic approach using her faith that offered a way to communicate with her. Our identical faith in God helped me assess her (rational and irrational) communication to understand her progress. During the first two sessions, I asked her to recite a scripture of my choice, and I would use the Bible to check if she recited it correctly. After reciting the scripture, she communicated to me what it meant. She knew all of the scriptures I chose, which amazed me even more. For the third session, she appeared elated to see me come to spend time with her. After the activity, I was able to address her talking to dead people on a daily basis. Ironically, when I addressed this, she named the dead loved ones and could tell me the dates they had died. It was her living children that she had problems remembering. The living children had stopped interacting and visiting, but in her mind her deceased husband and son visited her every day. For the fourth session, after the activity we addressed the need to attend the psychiatrist's appointments, take a bath, and wash her hair, which led to her shutting down. After a weekend visit from her living son, she no longer wanted to talk or see anyone. She also refused to get out of bed. Her physical and mental health were deteriorating. After several attempts to reconnect to no avail, the therapy was terminated.

However, I walked away knowing her trust in her faith. She believed her blessings were connected to this system of faith, which is grounded in Jesus Christ. In Him we have obtained an inheritance that is predestined according to the purpose of him who works all things according to counsel of his will. When you heard the word of truth, the gospel of your salvation, and believed in Him, these promises were sealed with the promised Holy Spirit, who is the guarantee of our inheritance until we acquire possession of it to the praise of his glory. (Ephesians 1: 11, 13, 14).

CONCLUSION

Faith shapes the essence of our existence more than we know. However, I must remain silent on the functioning of the brain because I have no workable knowledge nor understanding of what happens in the brain at various stages of life. Nevertheless, after thirty years as a therapist, I have learned that we really do not clearly understand how mental health plays out in the brain. We focus on treating symptoms of various mental health diagnoses. Mental health is as essential to living as physical health, therefore we must treat the whole person. I am of the opinion we consist of mind, body, and soul.

The soul is used synonymously with spirit and inner man, and is the essence of life. It is an essential part of life, such as feelings, thoughts, and actions in humans, and is regarded as a distinct entity from the body. It is the moral and emotional nature of human beings in which life is present, whether physical life or mental life. It is this spirit within the disabled senior that suffers the most, but that suffering goes unnoticed; therefore, the inner, emotional self goes untreated, affecting the physical and mental self. We all play roles in treating the disabled inner emotional suffering, including the ways we view, interact, and understand them.

As stated in the introduction, God is the source of our lives. God is the Potter who is molding disabled seniors who are seeking Him. It is God who is shaping us for our end-of-life experience. My hope is that readers walk away with a sense of urgency about understanding the emotional struggles of seniors and disabled seniors alike, which affects their mental state of being. These are people who, at various stages of life, were very active and viable in contributing to their communities and society in some shape or form. Remember, seniors struggle with not being able to think as fast as they used to, not remembering things like they used to, a need to be respected, and to not be taken for granted.

REFERENCES

Azrael/Meaning/Angel and Fate: https://www.britannica.com

Department of Health and Human Resources, West Virginia https://www.dhhr.wv.g

Department of Mental Health, World Health Organization, Geneva, Switzerland; 2008.

Holy Bible: English Standard Version, Copyright 2001

Rick Warren, The Purpose Driven Life; 2002.

Stanford Encyclopedia of Philosophy https://plato.stanford.edu/entries/faith Published June 23, 2010, revised March 30, 2016.

Swarthmore College: https://www.Swarthmore.edu